Fun Fan Facts:
The Unofficial NBA Edition

Memphis Grizzlies

Everything Young Memphis Grizzlies Fans Should Know

By: Jake Liam

Dedication

To every kid who ever got told they were in the wrong place at the wrong time. The Grizzlies started in the wrong city, played in the wrong market, and nobody gave them a chance. Then they moved to Memphis, built something nobody expected, and made the whole league feel it. Sometimes the wrong start leads to exactly the right story. Keep grinding.

THE NBA BY THE NUMBERS

MOST NBA CHAMPIONSHIPS*

- CELTICS (18) †
- LAKERS (17)
- WARRIORS (7)
- BULLS (6)
- SPURS (5)

As of the 2024-25 Season. † One Trophy = 4 Championships.

NBA HISTORY SNAPSHOT

1946 NBA Founded — **1954** Shot Clock Introduced — **1979** 3-Point Line Added — **2023** NBA Cup Introduced

BIG NUMBERS

$156 million
Stephen Curry's est. earnings in the 24-25 season

7'7"
Tallest player in NBA history (Gheorghe Mureșan & Manute Bol)

30 | 4 | 82

30 Teams Competing in the NBA

4 Playoff Rounds

82 Games Per Season

MEMPHIS GRIZZLIES
IN THE NBA

- FOUNDED: 1995 †
- NBA TITLES: 0
- CONFERENCE TITLES: 0*

14 Playoff Appearances

*† Founding dates are complicated & may cause arguments at Thanksgiving. Ask someone born before color TV. All Titles reflect pre-relocation franchise history. * As of 2024-25 Season.*

NBA ALL-TIME MVP LEADERS

KAREEM ABDUL-JABBAR (6) ★ MICHAEL JORDAN (5) ★ BILL RUSSELL (5)

EASTERN CONFERENCE

- Atlantic – **Celtics**
- Atlantic – **Nets**
- Atlantic – **Knicks**
- Atlantic – **76ers**
- Atlantic – **Raptors**
- Central – **Bulls**
- Central – **Cavaliers**
- Central – **Pistons**
- Central – **Pacers**
- Central – **Bucks**
- Southeast – **Hawks**
- Southeast – **Hornets**
- Southeast – **Heat**
- Southeast – **Magic**
- Southeast – **Wizards**

WESTERN CONFERENCE

- Pacific – **Lakers**
- Pacific – **Clippers**
- Pacific – **Warriors**
- Pacific – **Suns**
- Pacific – **Kings**
- Northwest – **Nuggets**
- Northwest – **Timberwolves**
- Northwest – **Thunder**
- Northwest – **Trail Blazers**
- Northwest – **Jazz**
- Southwest – **Mavericks**
- Southwest – **Rockets**
- Southwest – **Spurs**
- Southwest – **Pelicans**
- Southwest – **Grizzlies**

Introduction

Welcome, fans! Whether you are new to cheering for the Memphis Grizzlies or you have been grinding with the team your whole life, this book is packed with fun, exciting, and surprising facts about your favorite team. Get ready to impress your friends and family with everything you know about the Grizzlies.

Quick Timeout

FedExForum sits in the heart of downtown Memphis, just a short walk from Beale Street and some of the best barbecue on the planet.

When the Grizzlies are rolling, those nineteen thousand fans make enough noise to convince anyone within three blocks that something extremely important is happening. Because it is.

HOW IT WORKS

THE SEASON
82 Games. One Goal.
Each team plays 82 games.
Win enough to make the
Playoffs.
Every game counts!

PLAYOFFS
30 Teams. 16 Make It.
8 per conference make the playoffs.
Win=Advance | Lose=Go Home
Best record
gets home court!

PLAYOFF ROUNDS
Best of 7. Win 4 or Go Home.
4 rounds of pure pressure.
Every series is do-or-die!

OVERTIME?
5 More Minutes.
Keep playing until
someone pulls ahead.
No ties. Ever.

THE FINALS
One Series. One Champion.
Winner lifts the Trophy.
Legend status unlocked.

How the NBA Works

At first glance, basketball feels simple. Ten players. One ball. Two hoops. Go.

Then the NBA adds the layers.

An 82-game regular season. A draft where bad teams pick first. Playoffs that last two full months. Superstars who can change everything with one trade. Dynasties that rise, fall, and rise again.

And somehow, it all works.

The NBA is built on one big idea: every team gets a chance to reset, reload, and rise again. No relegation. No dropping down to a lower league. Just basketball, every night, from October through June.

It is a league designed for drama, stars, and comebacks. And once you understand the flow, it is impossible to stop watching.

The League Setup

The NBA has 30 teams, spread across the United States and Canada. Those teams are split into two conferences:

- Eastern Conference
- Western Conference

Each conference has three divisions, mostly based on geography. Divisions matter for scheduling, but not as much as they used to.

Every team plays 82 regular season games, usually from October through April. Home games. Road games. Back-to-back nights. Long road trips. The season is a marathon before the sprint even starts.

Win games, and you climb the standings. Lose too many, and the pressure builds fast.

How Games Are Played

An NBA game has four quarters, each lasting 12 minutes. That means 48 minutes of game time, plus timeouts, free throws, and the occasional coach argument that adds another 20 minutes nobody planned for.

Scoring is simple:

- A shot inside the three-point line is worth 2 points
- A shot beyond the arc is worth 3 points
- Free throws are worth 1 point

If the score is tied at the end of regulation, the game goes to overtime, which lasts 5 minutes. Still tied? Another overtime. Keep going until someone wins.

There is a shot clock too. Teams have 24 seconds to take a shot. No standing around. No holding the ball forever. Keep it moving.

The Regular Season Race

The regular season is long for a reason. It tests everything.

Depth. Health. Focus. Patience.

Teams play opponents from both conferences, but they face conference rivals more often. By the end of the season, each conference's top teams have earned their playoff spots the hard way.

The goal is simple: make the playoffs. But there is a twist.

The NBA Cup

In 2023, the NBA added something new to the middle of the season. Something with actual stakes. They called it the In-Season Tournament, now known as the NBA Cup.

It works like this: Every team plays a small group stage during November and December, with special court designs that look like nothing else in basketball. The best teams advance to a knockout round held in Las Vegas.

The winners split a prize pool. Players earn bonus money. And for the first time, a team could lift a trophy before the playoffs even started.

Some fans are still warming up to it. Some players love it. But the moment a team starts treating it seriously and a crowd shows up buzzing in December, it feels like something.

Which, honestly, sounds about right.

The Play-In Tournament

Instead of sending the top eight teams from each conference straight to the playoffs, the NBA added something new. The Play-In Tournament.

Here is how it works:

- Teams ranked 1 through 6 in each conference are safe
- Teams ranked 7 through 10 fight for the final two playoff spots

The 7 and 8 seeds have an advantage. Win once and you are in. Lose and you still get one more shot. The 9 and 10 seeds have to win twice in a row just to earn a first-round matchup.

It turns the end of the season into a sprint. Every game suddenly matters more. Fans love it. Coaches age rapidly.

The NBA Playoffs

Once the playoffs begin, everything tightens.

Sixteen teams enter. Eight from each conference. Every round is a best-of-seven games series. That means the first team to win four games moves on:

- First Round
- Conference Semifinals
- Conference Finals
- NBA Finals

Home-court advantage matters. Crowds get louder. Rotations get shorter. Superstars play heavier minutes. One bad quarter can flip a series. One great performance can define a career.

By the time the NBA Finals arrive in June, only two teams are left. One from the East. One from the West.

Four wins away from a championship. Four wins away from history.

The NBA Draft: Hope Begins Here

Here is where the NBA gets clever. Every summer, new players enter the league through the NBA Draft. Teams take turns selecting college players, international stars, and teenagers straight out of high school.

The teams that finished with the worst records get the best odds to pick early through the Draft Lottery. It is not guaranteed, but it gives struggling franchises a real shot at changing their future with one pick.

That means one bad season does not doom you forever. It might actually change everything. Some franchises are rebuilt by a single draft night moment.

Hope shows up wearing a new jersey.

No Relegation. All Pressure.

Unlike many global sports leagues, NBA teams never drop down to a lower league. They always stay in the NBA.

That does not mean there is no pressure.

Fans remember losing seasons. Owners make changes. Coaches get replaced. Players get traded. Every year is a test of direction, patience, and belief.

Stars, Systems, and Showtime

The NBA is famous for its stars. But stars do not win alone.

Teams need chemistry. Coaches need systems. Role players need to deliver on the biggest stages. One injury. One hot streak. One trade deadline deal. Any of it can flip a season.

That balance between individual brilliance and team basketball is what makes the league special.

Fast breaks. Buzzer-beaters. Game 7s. And moments that get replayed forever. That is the NBA.

Once you get the flow, it is pure electricity.

Memphis Grizzlies Facts

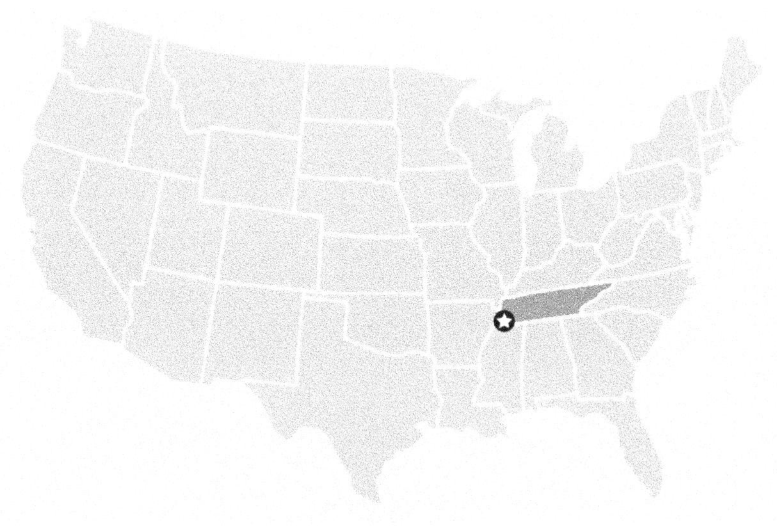

Home City

Memphis, Tennessee

Metro Area Population

About 1.4 Million

Home Arena

FedExForum

Max Capacity: 17,794

Conference / Division

Western Conference / Southwest Division

Famous Local Food

Memphis dry-rub BBQ ribs, pulled pork, fried catfish, banana pudding

Chapter 1: Born in the Wrong City

1. The Vancouver Experiment

In 1995, the NBA decided it was ready to go international. Not just with players from other countries, but with entire franchises planted on foreign soil. The league handed out two new expansion teams that year, and one of them landed in Vancouver, British Columbia, Canada. A professional NBA team. In Canada. In a city that had never hosted pro basketball before.

Vancouver was buzzing. The team needed a name, and organizers held a public contest. Thousands of entries poured in. The winner? Grizzlies. It made perfect sense for the Pacific Northwest, where grizzly bears roam the mountains and wilderness feels like it starts just past the city limits. The navy, teal, and copper color scheme looked sharp. The logo was bold. Everything about it said: we belong here.

The only problem was the basketball. The Grizzlies went 15 and 67 in their first season, which is the kind of record that makes your math teacher wince. But every franchise has to start somewhere, and Vancouver was officially on the NBA map. Imagine being a kid in British

Columbia, finally getting your own NBA team to root for. That feeling was real, even if the wins were not.

2. Grizzly Country

So why a grizzly bear? Because Vancouver sits right at the edge of some of the wildest wilderness in North America. British Columbia is home to thousands of grizzlies, and the bear is practically a symbol of the entire region. Picking the grizzly was not just a cool mascot decision. It was a statement about where the team came from and what it represented.

The original colors told the same story. Teal, copper, and deep blue. Colors that felt rugged, outdoorsy, and distinctly Canadian. Nothing about them screamed polished NBA franchise. They screamed mountains, rivers, and something untamed. For a brand-new team trying to carve out an identity, that was actually perfect.

Here is the fun part though. When the franchise eventually moved to Memphis, they kept the grizzly. Memphis, Tennessee does not have grizzly bears. The last wild grizzly in that part of the country disappeared from the American South well over a century ago. So Memphis ended up with a giant bear mascot that belongs, geographically speaking, about two thousand miles away. Nobody complained. The name was already too good to change.

3. Frozen Out

The Grizzlies struggled in Vancouver. That is putting it gently. Over six seasons, the team never finished above .500. They cycled through coaches, burned through draft picks, and watched their best young players get injured or traded before anything could be built. The city showed up early, curious and hopeful, but losing seasons have a way of emptying arenas.

The Canadian dollar was also working against them. Because the team earned revenue in Canadian currency but paid NBA salaries in American dollars, the financial math got painful fast. Signing free agents became nearly impossible when players realized they were taking a pay cut just by crossing the border. Other NBA teams could outbid Vancouver without even trying hard.

Attendance dropped. Local TV ratings softened. The energy that greeted the franchise in 1995 had mostly faded by 2000. Imagine planning a birthday party for six straight years and having fewer and fewer people show up each time. That was Vancouver Grizzlies basketball. The city did not fall out of love with the NBA. The situation just never gave them a real reason to fall in love in the first place.

4. Heading South

By 2001, the math was not working and the ownership knew it. The Vancouver Grizzlies were officially on the move. The NBA approved the relocation, and after a search for the right city, Memphis, Tennessee won the bid. The Grizzlies would play their first Memphis season in the Pyramid Arena, an actual giant pyramid sitting on the bank of the Mississippi River, while their permanent home was being built.

Memphis was not considered a glamour market. It was not Los Angeles or New York or Chicago. Skeptics wondered whether a mid-sized Southern city could support an NBA franchise long term. Memphis had other ideas. The city went after those tickets hard. Season ticket sales in the first year were strong enough to make the league pay attention. Memphis wanted professional basketball, and it was not shy about saying so.

The grizzly bear logo came with the team, and honestly it fit Memphis better than anyone expected. Because if there is one thing Memphis understands, it is toughness. The city has a blues-soaked, hardworking, never-back-down character that turned out to match the Grizzlies' personality almost perfectly. They were not supposed to thrive there. They absolutely did.

5. A Fresh Start

The Grizzlies' first few seasons in Memphis were still rebuilding years, but something felt different. The roster was young. The front office was drafting smart. And the city was loud in a way that Vancouver, toward the end, had not been. FedExForum, the team's brand-new permanent arena, opened in 2004 and gave Memphis a world-class building to match their world-class enthusiasm.

Then the 2001 NBA Draft happened, and a name that would reshape the entire franchise: Pau Gasol. He arrived as a 20-year-old from Spain and immediately started developing into a genuine star. Year by year, the Grizzlies were quietly assembling something.

That was fine. Memphis did not need anyone's attention yet. They were building the foundation for one of the most unique identities in the entire NBA. Toughness, team basketball, and a city that treated its players like family. The Vancouver years were a rough draft. Memphis was where the real story began.

6. Pau Gasol: The Spanish Star (2001-2008)

Pau Gasol arrived in Memphis at seven feet tall, speaking four languages, and playing basketball like someone had installed a European finishing school inside an NBA body. He was smooth. He was skilled. He could face up, post up, pass out of double teams, and hit mid-range jumpers that made defenders look like they had forgotten how to play defense entirely. Memphis had never seen anything quite like him.

Gasol won Rookie of the Year in 2002, which sounds obvious in hindsight but was genuinely surprising at the time. The Grizzlies were still a new franchise trying to figure out what they were. Pau gave them an answer. He was the guy. For seven seasons he carried Memphis on his very long, very talented back, making the playoffs, making All-Star teams, and making opponents deeply regret leaving him open near the elbow.

Then in 2008, he was traded to the Los Angeles Lakers for what many NBA historians still describe as the most lopsided deal since someone traded a sandwich for a sports car. The Lakers promptly won two championships. Memphis got some players whose names most Grizzlies fans immediately needed to look up. Pau Gasol remains beloved in Memphis, which says everything about how special those years were despite the ending.

7. Tony Allen: The Grindfather (2010-2017)

Tony Allen did not score 30 points a game. He did not have a signature sneaker. He was not on magazine covers. What Tony Allen did was make the best offensive player on the other team want to retire at halftime. He was the greatest perimeter defender of his generation, a heat-seeking missile in sneakers who turned guarding opponents into something that looked less like basketball and more like a nature documentary about a wolf following a deer.

His nickname, The Grindfather, was not handed to him by a marketing team. It was earned possession by possession, game by game, through seven seasons of absolute defensive relentlessness. Allen made guarding someone look personal. Like he had found out at breakfast that the guy he was covering had said something rude about Memphis, and he was going to spend 48 minutes reminding him of that.

Imagine going to work every single day and doing the most exhausting, least glamorous job in the office with more enthusiasm than anyone else in the building. That was Tony Allen. He was the engine underneath the Grit and Grind Grizzlies, the guy who set the temperature for the entire team every night. Memphis did not just like Tony Allen. Memphis became Tony Allen.

8. Zach Randolph: Z-Bo (2009-2017)

Zach Randolph is perhaps the most beloved Grizzly of all time, which is remarkable when you consider that he arrived in Memphis with a reputation that could most politely be described as complicated. He had bounced around the league. Critics doubted him. Coaches had concerns. Memphis said welcome home, handed him a basketball, and watched something beautiful happen.

Z-Bo became a monster. Not in a scary way. In the way that makes opposing power forwards call their families after games just to hear a friendly voice. He was a relentless scorer in the post, one of the best offensive rebounders the league had ever seen, and a physical presence so overwhelming that guarding him felt less like a basketball assignment and more like a personal test of character.

But the part nobody expected was how much Zach Randolph loved Memphis and how much Memphis loved him back. He ran basketball camps. He fed families at Thanksgiving. He became part of the city's fabric in a way that went way beyond wins and losses. When the Grizzlies were at their Grit and Grind peak, Z-Bo was the heartbeat. Loud, proud, and absolutely not interested in making your night easy.

9. Marc Gasol: The Anchor (2008-2019)

Here is something that sounds made up but is completely true. Pau and Marc Gasol are real brothers. Actual siblings. Same parents, same household, same dinner table in Spain. Their father Agusti Gasol played professional basketball in Spain, so the boys grew up in a home where basketball was basically a second language. Both sons turned out to be NBA-caliber big men. The odds of that happening are roughly the same as winning the lottery twice while being struck by lightning.

When Memphis traded Pau to the Lakers in 2008, Marc came back the other direction as part of the package. At the time Marc was young and largely unknown outside of Spain. The Lakers figured they were getting filler.

What they were actually doing was handing Memphis eleven more years of elite center play from the younger Gasol brother, which is the kind of gift you do not realize you have received until it is way too late to feel good about it.

Marc became one of the most complete centers of his generation, winning NBA Defensive Player of the Year in 2013 and an NBA Championship with Toronto in 2019. So Memphis had both Gasol brothers across different eras, got elite production from each of them, and the Lakers accidentally helped make it happen. The Gasols are the most famous brothers in NBA history, and Memphis got to claim both of them. Not bad for a city that started out with zero NBA history whatsoever.

Blake Griffin charges to the rim, but two defenders slam the door shut. Meet the Memphis Grizzlies during their famous Grit and Grind era. Marc Gasol and Zach Randolph made life miserable for opponents with tough defense and bruising play in the paint. Pretty basketball? Not always. Tough basketball? Absolutely. *Marc Gasol and Zach Randolph defend against Blake Griffin of the Los Angeles Clippers. Photograph via Wikimedia Commons. Licensed under CC BY-SA 2.0.*

10. Mike Conley: Mr. Grizzly (2007-2019)

Mike Conley was the fourth overall pick in the 2007 NBA Draft and spent twelve seasons in Memphis, which makes him the longest-tenured Grizzly in franchise history by a wide margin. He was quiet, professional, and consistently excellent in a way that somehow made people underrate him for most of his career. It became a running joke in basketball circles. Memphis had one of the best point guards in the league and half the country kept forgetting to mention him.

Conley made the All-Star team eventually, but for years he was the most underpaid and underappreciated star in the NBA. He averaged close to 20 points per game multiple times, ran the Grit and Grind offense with the precision of someone doing a very fast math problem while also playing defense, and never made a big scene about any of it. He just showed up, played at an elite level, and let the box scores do the talking.

In 2016 he signed a contract extension that was briefly the largest in NBA history, and the reaction from national media was something like surprise mixed with mild panic. Meanwhile, every single Grizzlies fan nodded calmly and said yes, obviously, that is exactly what Mike Conley is worth. He wore the Memphis uniform longer than any other player ever has. That is not just a fun fact. That is a statement about character.

Chapter 3: Grit, Grind, and Glory

11. The Greatest Upset

In the first round of the 2011 NBA Playoffs, the Memphis Grizzlies were seeded eighth. Dead last. The kind of seed that exists mostly so the bracket looks complete. Their opponent was the San Antonio Spurs, seeded first, led by Tim Duncan, and widely expected to dismantle Memphis with the calm, methodical efficiency of a man filing very organized paperwork. The Spurs had won four championships. The Grizzlies had never won a playoff series. This was going to be quick and painless. For the Spurs, anyway.

Nobody told Memphis that.

The Grizzlies won the series four games to two. They did not sneak through. They did not get lucky. They physically imposed their will on one of the greatest franchises in NBA history, game after game, until San Antonio had no answers left. Z-Bo averaged over 20 points and 12 rebounds. Marc Gasol was immovable. Tony Allen made Manu Ginobili look like he had forgotten how basketball worked. When the final buzzer sounded and Memphis had actually done it, grown adults in Tennessee were crying in their living rooms. A city that had been told for years it was too small, too quiet, too overlooked had just knocked out the number one seed in the entire Western Conference. Somewhere in Vancouver, a few old fans probably felt something too.

12. Grit and Grind: More Than a Motto

At some point during the early 2010s, a Memphis TV broadcaster said the words "grit and grind" to describe how the Grizzlies played, and the phrase attached itself to the franchise like a barnacle on a battleship. It was not a marketing slogan dreamed up in a conference room. It was a description. An accurate one.

The Grizzlies of that era played a style of basketball that was so physical, so defensively suffocating, so relentlessly exhausting for opponents that coaches around the league started scheduling extra recovery days before and after playing Memphis. Other teams had faster players. Other teams had better shooters. The Grizzlies had Tony Allen following your best player around like he had been personally assigned to ruin their evening, Z-Bo backing your power forward into the paint until they ran out of paint, and Marc Gasol

clogging the middle like a very intelligent, very large
traffic cone.

Imagine eating your least favorite meal for dinner every
single night for an entire season. That is what it felt like
to play the Grit and Grind Grizzlies. You were not going
to enjoy it. You were not going to look good doing it.
And you were definitely not going to feel great about
yourself when it was over. Memphis turned toughness
into an art form, and the whole league had to respect it
even while desperately wishing they did not have to
play them.

13. The 2013 Playoff Run

The 2012-13 Memphis Grizzlies were built different.
They finished the regular season strong, entered the
playoffs with genuine confidence, and in the first round
dispatched the Los Angeles Clippers in six games. That
alone was worth celebrating. But what came next was
the kind of basketball that makes people stop whatever
they are doing and just watch.

In the second round, Memphis faced the Oklahoma City
Thunder. Kevin Durant. One of the most talented
offensive rosters the Western Conference had
assembled in years, even without an injured Russell

Westbrook. The Grizzlies beat them four games to one. They did not just win. They made a super-team look uncomfortable in ways that a roster with that much talent should never look uncomfortable.

Memphis eventually lost to the San Antonio Spurs in the Western Conference Finals, which stings even now. But that 2013 run proved something permanent. This was not a fluke franchise. This was not a team that stumbled into success by accident. The Grit and Grind Grizzlies were legitimate contenders, and the conference finals trophy case still has a Spurs-shaped dent in it from where Memphis knocked on the door so hard.

14. Mike Conley's Historic Contract

In the summer of 2016, Mike Conley signed a contract extension worth 153 million dollars over five years. At the moment of signing, it was the largest contract in NBA history. The most money ever guaranteed to a basketball player up to that point in the entire history of the sport. And the national reaction was, to put it kindly, bewildered.

Sports radio melted down. Columnists wrote think pieces. People who had never once watched a

Memphis Grizzlies game in their lives suddenly had very strong opinions about whether Mike Conley deserved 153 million dollars. The short answer is yes. The longer answer is that Mike Conley had spent nine seasons being quietly elite while the basketball world looked directly at him and somehow saw nothing. He was the engine of a perennial playoff team. He was one of the best point guards in the conference. He was so consistently good that people had apparently mistaken consistency for ordinariness.

Here is the part that might actually make you tear up a little. Conley had heard the doubts his entire career. Not good enough. Not flashy enough. Not the guy. He never complained. He never forced shots to boost his stats. He just played the right way, every night, for nine years, and let Memphis see exactly who he was. When that contract landed, it was not just money. It was the NBA finally saying out loud what Memphis fans had known for nearly a decade. Mike Conley was worth every penny and then some.

15. The 2022 Playoff Statement

The 2021-22 Memphis Grizzlies finished the regular season as the second seed in the entire Western Conference. Let that settle in. A team with an average age that made some rosters look like a retirement community by comparison had just posted 56 wins and earned home court advantage in the playoffs against franchises with far more experience, far more hardware, and far more people picking them to win.

Ja Morant was 22 years old and playing like someone had given a video game character an actual body. Jaren Jackson Jr. was locking down opposing bigs with a defensive instinct that seemed unfair for someone his age. The whole roster played with a fearlessness that was either inspiring or terrifying depending on which bench you were sitting on. Memphis hammered the Minnesota Timberwolves in the first round. They pushed the Golden State Warriors to six games in the second round before bowing out.

The loss hurt. But the season said something that could not be unsaid. The Grit and Grind era had passed, and what replaced it was not a rebuilding project or a quiet transition period. What replaced it was something potentially even better. A young, explosive, hungry team in a city that had waited through Vancouver expansion drafts and empty arenas and lopsided trades for exactly this moment. Memphis did not just make the playoffs in 2022. Memphis announced that the next great chapter was already being written, and it was going to be loud.

16. Grizz the Mascot

The Memphis Grizzlies' mascot is a giant fuzzy bear named Grizz, and he is one of the most unhinged entertainers in professional sports. Not unhinged in a concerning way. Unhinged in the way where you watch him do a full backflip off a trampoline into a foam pit during a timeout and think, that bear has genuinely no fear of consequences whatsoever. He has been doing this for years. He has not slowed down. If anything he has escalated.

Grizz consistently ranks among the top mascots in the entire NBA, which is a competitive field full of large, costumed animals doing increasingly ridiculous things to keep fans entertained during stoppages in play. Grizz wins because he commits fully. There is no halfway with this bear. He is either doing something spectacular or plotting something spectacular, and both options are compelling television.

The funniest part is that grizzly bears in real life are enormous, dangerous, and deeply uninterested in entertaining anyone. They eat, they sleep, they occasionally demolish things. The Memphis version has a Twitter account, a signature dance move, and has probably high-fived more humans in a single season than a wild grizzly encounters in a lifetime. Nature did not make Grizz. Memphis did. And Memphis made him better.

17. FedExForum

The Memphis Grizzlies play their home games at FedExForum, which opened in 2004 and immediately became one of the loudest buildings in the NBA. The name comes from FedEx, the global shipping and logistics company that is headquartered right there in Memphis. This is fitting because FedEx built its entire business model around delivering things fast and on time, and the Grizzlies built their entire identity around delivering pain, also fast, and also very much on time.

FedExForum sits in the heart of downtown Memphis, which means it is a short walk from Beale Street, world-class barbecue, and live blues music on basically any night of the week. Before and after games, the surrounding area turns into one big celebration. Other NBA arenas are in nice locations. FedExForum is in a neighborhood that feels like it was specifically designed to make sports more fun.

The arena holds just under nineteen thousand people, and when Memphis is rolling, those nineteen thousand people make enough noise to convince anyone within a three-block radius that something extremely important is happening. Which it is. Visiting teams have described playing at FedExForum during a playoff game as one of the most hostile environments in basketball. The Grizzlies consider that a compliment. It absolutely is one.

18. The Growl Towel

At some point someone in the Memphis Grizzlies organization handed fans a towel and said wave this, and fans said okay, and now it is a sacred ritual. The Growl Towel is a simple white towel with the Grizzlies logo on it, distributed to fans on big game nights, and when nineteen thousand people start spinning them simultaneously the effect is somewhere between a blizzard and a collective nervous breakdown for whoever is trying to inbound the ball for the other team.

The towel tradition is not unique to Memphis, but Memphis does it with a particular intensity that feels personal. Like every single person in that building has a specific grievance against the visiting team and the towel is the most socially acceptable way to express it. You cannot do anything alarming in a public arena. You can absolutely windmill a small white towel with maximum aggression.

Visiting players have mentioned the towels in postgame interviews. Not in a nice way. In the way where you can tell they were slightly unnerved by nineteen thousand synchronized towels spinning in their direction for three hours. If you ever go to a Grizzlies playoff game and someone hands you a Growl Towel at the door, you spin that thing like your life depends on it. Because in Memphis, game nights kind of feel like they do.

19. Memphis Music and the Team's DNA

Memphis is one of the most musically significant cities in the entire world, and that is not an exaggeration. Beale Street is one of the most important homes of the blues. Sun Studio is where Elvis Presley, Johnny Cash, and Jerry Lee Lewis all recorded within a few years of each other, which is the kind of coincidence that makes you wonder if something was in the water. Stax Records gave the world Otis Redding and Isaac Hayes. The city did not just contribute to American music. It basically wrote several of the most important chapters.

That musical DNA seeped into the Grizzlies' identity in ways both obvious and subtle. The team plays in a city where struggle is taken seriously, where soul is not a buzzword but a lived experience, and where toughness is something people wear quietly rather than announce loudly. That is exactly how the Grit and Grind Grizzlies played. No announcements. Just results. Otis Redding would have appreciated the work ethic. Elvis would have appreciated the arena energy. Isaac Hayes would have written a very dramatic orchestral piece about the 2011 Spurs upset, and it would have been incredible.

The connection between the music and the basketball is not just poetic. It is real. Memphis fans bring a rhythm to their arenas the way Memphis musicians bring feel to a recording studio. You cannot fake either one. You either have it or you do not. Memphis has always had it.

20. BBQ Capital of the World

Memphis will fight you about barbecue. Politely, but firmly, and with a level of conviction that suggests they have been preparing for this argument their entire lives. Memphis-style barbecue means slow-smoked pork, dry rub seasoning, and a philosophy that views sauce as something you can have on the side if you absolutely must, but which the meat should not need if it was done correctly. This stance is deeply held and non-negotiable.

The city has legendary BBQ joints that have been operating for decades, drawing visitors from across the country who fly specifically to Memphis to eat ribs and then fly home again. That is a real thing people do. The World Championship Barbecue Cooking Contest, held annually in Memphis, is one of the largest barbecue competitions on the planet. Hundreds of teams. Thousands of attendees. A level of seriousness about smoked meat that would impress a panel of international diplomats.

The Grizzlies and Memphis BBQ share more than a zip code. They share a personality. Both are unpretentious, both are built on a slow process done right rather than shortcuts, and both have made people who initially underestimated them deeply regret that decision. You do not walk into a Memphis BBQ joint expecting anything fancy and you do not walk into FedExForum expecting a soft game. What you get in both places is something real, something earned, and something you will absolutely be thinking about on the drive home.

21. Ja Morant: The #2 Pick Who Changed Everything

Ja Morant was selected second overall in the 2019 NBA Draft and immediately made everyone wonder why the conversation had taken this long to find him. He played college ball at Murray State, which is a small school in Kentucky that most NBA scouts drive past on their way to watch players at bigger programs. Ja was putting up 25 points and 10 assists per game and basically waving a giant flag, and the league still needed a moment to fully register what it was looking at.

Memphis took him second and handed him the keys immediately. He responded by winning Rookie of the Year in his first season, becoming one of the youngest players in NBA history to post a 40-point triple-double, and generally playing with an athleticism so extreme that highlights of him became the kind of thing people texted to friends at midnight with the message watch this right now. His dunks do not look like basketball plays. They look like someone bet him he could not do that and he took it personally.

Imagine being an opposing defender, having done your film study, having your coach explain the game plan, feeling genuinely prepared, and then watching Ja Morant leave the floor from a position where leaving the floor should not be physically possible. Then he lands, the arena explodes, and you still have forty minutes of game left. That is the experience of guarding Ja Morant. Multiple defenders have checked their shoes afterward just to make sure they were wearing the right ones.

22. Jaren Jackson Jr.: Defensive Player of the Year

Jaren Jackson Jr. is seven feet tall, can shoot threes at a high level, runs the floor like someone who did not get the memo about being seven feet tall, and in the 2022-23 season won NBA Defensive Player of the Year. He was 23 years old. He blocked shots at a rate that made opponents rethink their entire approach to the paint before they even crossed halfcourt. Some players changed their shot selection just by walking through the FedExForum tunnel and remembering who was waiting for them.

The Defensive Player of the Year award goes to the player who, above everyone else in the league, made life genuinely miserable for people trying to score near him. JJJ won it convincingly, which means a roomful of NBA professionals looked at all the evidence and agreed that Jaren Jackson Jr. was the most difficult human being in basketball to score against. That is a spectacular thing to be when you are 23.

Here is what makes it even better. JJJ is not just a defensive specialist who happens to play offense. He can stretch the floor, hit big shots, and make plays in late-game situations when the whole building knows the ball is coming to him. He is a complete player who also happened to lead the league in total blocks in 2022-23. He is essentially a Swiss Army knife that someone accidentally made seven feet long. Memphis drafted him fourth overall in 2018 and has been extremely pleased with that decision ever since.

23. The 2021-22 Season

The 2021-22 Memphis Grizzlies won 56 games, finished second in the Western Conference, and did it with a roster whose average age was young enough that several players could not legally rent a car without a surcharge. This is remarkable. Most 56-win teams are built around veterans who have been through playoff runs, learned hard lessons, and accumulated the kind of scar tissue that makes you harder to rattle. Memphis was built around guys who were still finding out what kind of scar tissue they were going to develop.

Ja Morant won Most Improved Player that season and finished top five in MVP voting. The team won a first-round playoff series against the Timberwolves with the kind of swagger that made neutral fans grin. Then they pushed the eventual champion Golden State Warriors to six games in the second round, which was not supposed to happen and happened anyway, because Memphis refusing to do what it is supposed to do is basically a franchise tradition at this point.

The season mattered beyond the wins and losses. It told a story about what this franchise had become. Not a cute young team getting experience. A genuine threat. The kind of team that other franchises' fans check the bracket for immediately, not because they are rooting for Memphis but because they want to know if their team has to play them. That is respect. The Grizzlies have been earning it since 2001, and the 2021-22 version collected the full payment.

24. Memphis as a Basketball City

Before the Grizzlies arrived, Memphis already had basketball in its bones. Penny Hardaway, one of the most gifted and stylish point guards of the 1990s, grew up right there in Memphis. He starred at the University of Memphis, became an NBA superstar with the Orlando Magic, and eventually came back home to coach college basketball at his alma mater. The city did not need the NBA to teach it about basketball. The NBA showed up and found a city that already knew.

The University of Memphis has produced NBA players for decades. The program has been a national powerhouse at various points, drawing local talent and giving Memphis fans something to cheer for long before the Grizzlies arrived. When the NBA franchise landed in 2001, it did not have to build a fan base from scratch. It plugged into an existing current.

That basketball history matters because it means Memphis fans are not casual. They know the game. They understand what they are watching. They appreciate defense, they recognize when a team is playing the right way, and they respond to authenticity over flash. This is partly why the Grit and Grind era connected so deeply. Memphis fans did not need the team to be glamorous. They needed the team to be real. The Grizzlies were as real as it gets, and the city has never let them forget it.

25. The Road Ahead

The Memphis Grizzlies are one of the most interesting franchises in basketball right now, which is a sentence that would have genuinely confused someone in 2000 if you had traveled back in time to tell them. A team that started in Vancouver with fifteen wins and a color scheme inspired by Canadian wilderness is now a cornerstone franchise with a transcendent young star, a defensive anchor, and a city behind them that treats home games like civic events.

Ja Morant's ceiling is one of the most debated topics in the entire sport. When healthy and locked in, he is a legitimate MVP-level player, the kind of talent that shows up a handful of times per generation and reshapes how the position is understood. Jaren Jackson Jr. is building a case as one of the best two-way big men in the league. The supporting pieces around them have enough youth and potential to suggest that this window is not closing anytime soon.

Memphis has been through the expansion struggles and the relocation and the lopsided trades and the years when nobody outside Tennessee was paying attention. They have been the underdog and the upset and the team that makes you feel something even when they lose. They have gone from a footnote to a chapter to, increasingly, a headline. The road ahead for the Grizzlies looks like the best version of the story that started back in Vancouver all those years ago. Longer. Louder. And nowhere near finished.

Bonus Trivia Quiz!

You think you are a true Memphis Grizzlies fan? Try this bonus quiz!

1. In what year did the Vancouver Grizzlies play their first NBA season?

A) 1993
B) 1995
C) 1997
D) 1999

2. How did the Grizzlies get their name?

A) The owner's favorite animal was a grizzly bear
B) Fans voted in a public naming contest
C) The NBA assigned the name during expansion
D) It was named after a local Vancouver sports legend

3. What arena did the Memphis Grizzlies play in during their first season in Tennessee?

A) FedExForum
B) The Rose Garden
C) The Pyramid Arena
D) Staples Center

4. Which award did Pau Gasol win in his first NBA season with Memphis?

A) MVP
B) Most Improved Player
C) Defensive Player of the Year
D) Rookie of the Year

5. What made signing free agents in Vancouver so financially difficult for the Grizzlies?

A) The arena was too small to generate revenue
B) NBA salaries were paid in US dollars but revenue came in Canadian dollars
C) Vancouver had no corporate sponsors willing to invest
D) The ownership group ran out of money after the first season

6. Pau and Marc Gasol are brothers. What did their father do professionally?

A) He was a professional soccer player in Spain
B) He was a professional basketball player in Spain
C) He was a coach for the Spanish national team
D) He was a sports journalist who covered the NBA

7. What nickname did Memphis fans give Tony Allen?

A) The Enforcer
B) The Grindmaster
C) The Grindfather
D) The Wall

8. The 2011 Grizzlies pulled off one of the greatest upsets in NBA playoff history. Which top-seeded team did they defeat?

A) Los Angeles Lakers
B) Oklahoma City Thunder
C) Dallas Mavericks
D) San Antonio Spurs

9. When Mike Conley signed his contract extension in 2016, what made it historically significant?

A) It was the first max contract ever given to a point guard
B) It was briefly the largest contract in NBA history
C) It was the longest contract the Grizzlies had ever offered
D) It included the first no-trade clause in franchise history

10. What global company headquartered in Memphis gives FedExForum its name?

A) A shipping and logistics company
B) A pharmaceutical company
C) An airline
D) A technology company

11. What is the name of the Grizzlies' official mascot?

A) Growl
B) Memphis
C) Grizz
D) Bear

12. Where was Ja Morant playing college basketball before the Grizzlies drafted him second overall in 2019?

A) University of Kentucky
B) University of Tennessee
C) Duke University
D) Murray State University

13. Which award did Jaren Jackson Jr. win during the 2022-23 NBA season?

A) Most Improved Player
B) Defensive Player of the Year
C) Sixth Man of the Year
D) Most Valuable Player

14. Memphis is considered the birthplace of which music genre?

A) Jazz
B) Country
C) The Blues
D) Rock and Roll

15. In the 2021-22 season, how many games did the Memphis Grizzlies win to finish as the second seed in the Western Conference?

A) 48
B) 52
C) 56
D) 60

Super Fan Secret Challenge

Only a true Memphis Grizzlies fan will know this.

(No Answer Provided)

The Grizzlies' famous "Grit and Grind" phrase was not invented by the front office or a marketing team. It came from somewhere much more organic. Where did the phrase actually originate, and who said it first?

A) Zach Randolph used it in a postgame press conference after the 2011 Spurs upset
B) A Memphis TV broadcaster used it during a game broadcast and it caught on immediately
C) Tony Allen had it printed on a custom t-shirt that went viral locally
D) Head coach Lionel Hollins said it in his opening press conference when he took the job

Answer Key

1. B) 1995

2. B) Fans voted in a public naming contest

3. C) The Pyramid Arena

4. D) Rookie of the Year

5. B) NBA salaries were paid in US dollars but revenue came in Canadian dollars

6. B) He was a professional basketball player in Spain

7. C) The Grindfather

8. D) San Antonio Spurs

9. B) It was briefly the largest contract in NBA history

10. A) A shipping and logistics company

11. C) Grizz

12. D) Murray State University

13. B) Defensive Player of the Year

14. C) The Blues

15. C) 56

NBA PLAYOFF BRACKET

First Round	Semifinals	Conf. Finals	Finals	Conf. Finals	Semifinals	First Round

* Fill in your picks and try not to argue with your friends about it!

Part of the Fun Fan Facts: The Unofficial Sports Guide Series

Be the Boss of the Playoffs

You've broken down the matchups. You know which superstar takes over in the fourth quarter. You've seen the bench units that quietly decide series. You've watched the adjustments coaches make when their backs are against the wall.

Now it's time to stop watching and start deciding.

On this page, you are not just a fan. You are the Head Coach drawing up the last play with three seconds left on the clock. You are the GM who built this roster. You are the analyst who saw it all coming.

This is not just filling out a bracket.

This is building your championship run.

Sixteen teams enter the NBA Playoffs. The path is brutal. Best of seven. No shortcuts. No hiding. Every round gets louder, harder, and more personal.

This bracket is your Playoff Control Room.

The Game Plan

1. Survive Round One: Start with the opening round. Which matchup is going seven games? Who has the closer? Who folds under pressure? Make the calls.

2. Feel the Momentum: As you move into the Conference Semifinals and Conference Finals, things change. Role players become heroes. Stars feel the weight. Trust your reads.

3. Own the Finals: Trace your picks all the way to the NBA Finals. When the confetti falls and the trophy is raised, you'll find out who earned it.

House Rules: Circle your boldest upset. That is your official "I knew it" moment.

Choose Your Weapon: Pencil if you want flexibility. Pen if you trust your instincts. Sharpie if you believe in chaos.

Because once the playoffs tip off, there is no rewinding Game 7.

Make your picks. Trust your basketball brain. And let the playoff drama begin.

Fun Facts Wrap-Up

You made it through! You're officially a true superfan! Now it's time to put your knowledge to the test. Share these facts with friends and see who really knows their team best.

Love the series?

Your reviews help other fans discover Fun Fan Facts. If you enjoyed this book, we'd really appreciate you sharing your thoughts and leaving a review.

Want more Fun Fan Facts?

Scan the QR code below to visit our site and explore bonus trivia, challenges, and special extras - including new teams, future series, and collectible fun as they're released.

Collect All the Fun Fan Facts Series!

Check off every book you read. See the full set on Amazon. Search "Fun Fan Facts Jake Liam."

World Cup 2026 Edition

☐ Algeria   ☐ France   ☐ Paraguay

☐ Argentina   ☐ Germany   ☐ Portugal

☐ Australia   ☐ Ghana   ☐ Qatar

☐ Austria   ☐ Haiti   ☐ Saudi Arabia

☐ Belgium   ☐ Iran   ☐ Scotland

☐ Brazil   ☐ Ivory Coast   ☐ Senegal

☐ Canada   ☐ Japan   ☐ South Africa

☐ Cape Verde   ☐ Jordan   ☐ South Korea

☐ Colombia   ☐ Mexico   ☐ Spain

☐ Croatia   ☐ Morocco   ☐ Switzerland

☐ Curaçao   ☐ Netherlands   ☐ Tunisia

☐ Ecuador   ☐ New Zealand   ☐ United States

☐ Egypt   ☐ Norway   ☐ Uruguay

☐ England   ☐ Panama   ☐ Uzbekistan

World Cup 2026 Group Edition

☐ Group A   ☐ Group E   ☐ Group I

☐ Group B   ☐ Group F   ☐ Group J

☐ Group C   ☐ Group G   ☐ Group K

☐ Group D   ☐ Group H   ☐ Group L

English Football Edition

- ☐ Arsenal F.C.
- ☐ Aston Villa F.C.
- ☐ Chelsea F.C.
- ☐ Everton F.C.
- ☐ Fulham F.C.
- ☐ Liverpool F.C.
- ☐ Manchester City
- ☐ Manchester United
- ☐ Newcastle United F.C.
- ☐ Tottenham Hotspur
- ☐ West Ham United
- ☐ Wrexham A.F.C.

NBA Edition

- ☐ Atlanta Hawks
- ☐ Boston Celtics
- ☐ Brooklyn Nets
- ☐ Charlotte Hornets
- ☐ Chicago Bulls
- ☐ Cleveland Cavaliers
- ☐ Dallas Mavericks
- ☐ Denver Nuggets
- ☐ Detroit Pistons
- ☐ Golden State Warriors
- ☐ Houston Rockets
- ☐ Indiana Pacers
- ☐ LA Clippers
- ☐ Los Angeles Lakers
- ☐ Memphis Grizzlies
- ☐ Miami Heat
- ☐ Milwaukee Bucks
- ☐ Minnesota Timberwolves
- ☐ New Orleans Pelicans
- ☐ New York Knicks
- ☐ Oklahoma City Thunder
- ☐ Orlando Magic
- ☐ Philadelphia 76ers
- ☐ Phoenix Suns
- ☐ Portland Trail Blazers
- ☐ Sacramento Kings
- ☐ San Antonio Spurs
- ☐ Toronto Raptors
- ☐ Utah Jazz
- ☐ Washington Wizards

About the Author

Jake is a 13-year-old sports fan who loves football, American football, and basketball. He plays soccer as a goalie and dreams of one day playing for West Ham United and helping teach kids to love the game. His passion for sports runs in the family - his dad was a professional baseball player, and his stepdad sparked his love for West Ham. Through the Fun Fan Facts series, he shares the fun and excitement of sports with fans everywhere.